Sound Trackers

Soul

Brunning, Bob
Soul. - (Soundtrackers)
1. Soul music - Juvenile literature
2. Soul musicians - Juvenile literature
I. Title
781.6'44

Printed and bound in Italy

Soul

Bob Brunning

CONTENTS

INTRODUCTION 5

JAMES BROWN 6

RAY CHARLES 8

ARETHA FRANKLIN 10

MARVIN GAYE 12

WHITNEY HOUSTON 14

The JACKSONS 16

WILSON PICKETT 18

OTIS REDDING 20

SMOKEY ROBINSON 22

DIANA ROSS 24

IKE and TINA TURNER 26

STEVIE WONDER 28

GAZETTEER 30

INDEX 32

On these discs is a selection of the artist's recordings. Many of these albums are now available on CD. If they are not, many of the tracks from them can be found on compilation CDs.

These boxes give you extra information about the artists and their times.

Some contain anecdotes about the artists themselves or about the people who helped their careers or, occasionally, about those who exploited them.

Others provide historical facts about the music, lifestyle, fans, fads and fashions of the day.

INTRODUCTION

'Soul music' is a very broad term, used to describe the popular music of black America, which emerged in the late 1950s and early '60s. Its roots were in light jazz and the gospel music that was heard in churches all over the country. Over the next 40 years, soul changed out of all recognition, as pioneers such as Smokey Robinson and Stevie Wonder set new standards with their songwriting and production.

Richard Roundtree (above) starred in the 1971 'blaxploitation' film 'Shaft'. 'Blaxploitation' means the exploitation of black people by producers of black-oriented films. Soul star Isaac Hayes (left) won an Oscar for the title song.

There were four major soul labels in the 1960s and '70s, each of which had a unique sound. The most famous was Motown in Detroit, which still exists today, but as a small part of a much larger company. Motown mostly recruited local talent, but Atlantic in New York searched far and wide to find stars such as Aretha Franklin and Ray Charles. Stax, in the southern city of Memphis, was always associated with the funky, good-time sound of Booker T and the MGs and Isaac Hayes. Philadelphia International Records (PIR) was as important to soul in the 1970s as Motown had been in the '60s. PIR had Teddy Pendergrass, the O'Jays and the Three Degrees on its books.

But soul was not all about having fun. It gave a voice to a new generation of black Americans, who were angry at the way they were treated, but proud of their heritage. Compared to jazz or blues, soul is a young form of music. Who knows how it will develop in the next 40 years?

JAMES BROWN

The Godfather of Soul, Mr Dynamite, Soul Brother Number One, The Hardest-Working Man in Show Business – just some of the descriptions given to James Brown, the singer whose career has spanned nearly half a century. But for all his drive, business-sense and the praise heaped upon him, James has always been an unpredictable genius, who has often fallen foul of the law.

'Please, Please, Please' 1959
'Live At The Apollo' 1963
'Sex Machine' 1970
'Hot Pants' 1971
'There It Is' 1972

'Payback' 1973
'Black Caesar' 1973
'Hell' 1974
'In The Jungle Mood' 1986
'Soul Jubilee' 1999
'Legends Collection' 2001

JUVENILE DELINQUENT

Born in South Carolina in 1933, James was already in trouble in his teens, doing time in a corrective institution for armed robbery. The family of singer Bobby Byrd helped to gain him parole, and James and Bobby started a gospel group. The group changed direction to rhythm and blues (R&B), called themselves the Famous Flames, signed to the Federal label and had a hit with 'Please, Please, Please'. It looked like the band was destined for stardom, but their next nine records flopped.

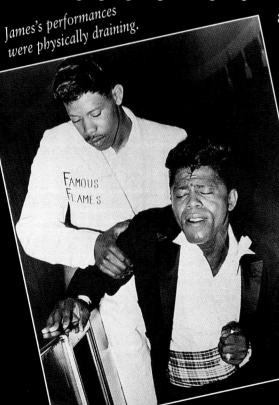

James's performances were physically draining.

HARD WORK PAYS OFF

But James showed superhuman determination, touring relentlessly, sharpening his act and keeping an eye on changing trends. After no hits for two years, Federal was about to drop the band when 'Try Me' hit No. 1 in the R&B charts in 1958. Now the focal point of the band, James took a large group of musicians on the road. His shows were a mixture of hysteria and musical precision, and as the 1960s dawned, James's R&B became harder, as he tried out Latin and jazz rhythms.

THE APOLLO

The Apollo Theater in Harlem, New York, has been a centre for musical talent since 1913. Originally it was called Hurtig and Seamon's New (Burlesque) Theater, and it provided variety entertainment for mainly white audiences. Since 1935, the Apollo has been host to almost every major black performer, including James Brown, jazz singer Ella Fitzgerald, blues legend Bessie Smith, rock star Prince, and the soul musicians listed in the picture below.

The city of New York has listed the interior and exterior of the Apollo Theater as designated landmarks.

By 1963, James was well-known for his tortured, screaming voice and manic stage shows, but it was only in June of that year that he became a superstar. That month saw the release of his 'Live At The Apollo' album, recorded at the famous Harlem venue the previous year. The record managed to capture the excitement and intensity of a James Brown performance, and it hit No. 2 in the US pop charts – an astonishing feat for a heavy soul disc.

A NEW GENERATION OF FANS

James built on the success of 'Live At The Apollo' with a string of hits which defined 1960s soul – 'Papa's Got A Brand New Bag', 'I Got You (I Feel Good)' and 'Say It Loud – I'm Black And I'm Proud'. The hits were drying up by the mid-1970s, but he found new fans in the '80s and '90s when dozens of rap and hip-hop artists sampled his earlier work. James was jailed for firearms offences in 1988. Free again in 1991, he hit the stage once more.

James Brown is well-known for his flamboyant stage outfits.

RAY CHARLES

At the dawn of the 1960s, the expression 'soul music' had not been invented. Ray Charles probably did more to develop the music than any other musician. He combined the high-powered R&B of the '50s with elements of gospel music, country, jazz and blues, to create a fresh and exciting new sound.

'The Genius Of Ray Charles' 1959
'The Genius Hits The Road' 1960
'Modern Sounds In Country And Western Music' 1962
'Sweet & Sour Tears' 1964

'Live' 1973
'Anthology' 1989
'Very Best Of Ray Charles, Vols 1 & 2' 2000
'Cocktail Hour' 2001
'Confession Blues' 2001

A DIFFICULT START

Ray Charles Robinson had a tough childhood. He went blind at the age of six, and by the time he was 17, both his parents were dead. But Ray had studied composition and had learned to play a number of instruments at the St Augustine School for the Deaf and the Blind. So, despite being orphaned at an early age, he was able to fend for himself, and start a career as a musician. In 1949, aged 18, he signed to Downbeat Records.

Ray Charles is sometimes accused of being a showbiz sell-out.

SIGNED BY ATLANTIC

Ray's biggest influence was the gentle crooner and pianist Nat 'King' Cole, and his early recordings never hint at the rough, emotional style he would later adopt. In 1952, his recording contract was bought out by Atlantic Records. Ray hit No. 7 in the R&B charts with 'It Should Have Been Me', the first in a string of hits for Atlantic, where his sound got harder. And the hits kept on coming – 'What'd I Say', 'Georgia On My Mind' and Ray's first No. 1 on the pop charts, 'Hit The Road, Jack', in 1961.

INTERNATIONAL STAR

By the mid-1960s, Ray was a major star, with another No. 1 to his name – 'I Can't Stop Loving You'. He was introducing hints of gospel music to his work, and inventing his own brand of soul. His triumphant career was only interrupted by an arrest for drug possession in 1966 – a medical check-up, showing him to be drug-free, kept him out of jail. For the next 35 years, garlanded with awards and feted all over the world, Ray has proven himself to have one of the most distinctive voices in soul music.

ATLANTIC RECORDS

Along with Stax, Motown and Philadelphia International, Atlantic was one of the big four soul record labels. Ahmet Ertegun, son of the former Turkish ambassador to the United States, borrowed $10,000 from his dentist to start the New York-based label in 1947. The investment soon paid off – along with Ray Charles, Atlantic had the Coasters, Aretha Franklin, Wilson Pickett and Solomon Burke on its books. From the 1960s, Atlantic branched out into rock music, signing Led Zeppelin and AC/DC.

Ahmet Ertegun (right) with Jack Bruce of Cream, one of the first rock acts to be signed by Atlantic.

Ray Charles founded his own record label, Tangerine, in 1966.

ARETHA FRANKLIN

Aretha Franklin, the Queen of Soul, was arguably the most exciting singer to burst on to the soul scene in the 1960s. Her powerful and emotional vocal range has made her the most recognizable female singer in black music. It was in church that she discovered her voice.

GOSPEL BEGINNINGS

Aretha was the fourth child of the Reverend C.L. Franklin, Pastor of the New Bethel Church in Detroit, who was the most famous gospel preacher of the 1950s. He spotted his daughter's potential, and promoted her as a soloist in the choir, turning young Aretha into a local celebrity. She made her first gospel recordings at the age of 14. This brought Aretha to the attention of Columbia Records, who signed her when she was 18, in 1960.

'Aretha Arrives' 1967
'Lady Soul' 1968
'Aretha Now' 1968
'Soul '69' 1969
'Spirit In The Dark' 1970

'Young, Gifted And Black' 1971
'Amazing Grace' 1972
'Who's Zoomin' Who?' 1985
'A Rose Is Still A Rose' 1998
'Love Songs' 2001

ARETHA ARRIVES

Aretha was unhappy with the way she was treated by Columbia, and when her contract expired in 1966, she was snapped up by Atlantic. Producer Jerry Wexler was the first person to capture the true Aretha Franklin sound, and success arrived at last. 'I Never Loved A Man (The Way I Love You)' topped the R&B charts for nine weeks, and 'Respect' was No. 1 in the pop charts for a month. 'Think' and 'I Say A Little Prayer' sealed Aretha's reputation as the purest voice in soul.

AMAZING GRACE

After several years recording non-religious material, Aretha returned to her gospel roots in 1972. The result was the inspiring double album, 'Amazing Grace', recorded in a Los Angeles church. Aretha spent the next 30 years balancing gospel with raw soul music, and collected over a dozen Grammy awards and countless gold discs along the way. Tragedy struck in 1985, when Aretha's father was shot during a civil rights campaign. He survived, but remained in a coma until his death in 1987, just as Aretha was enjoying her last US and UK No. 1 – 'I Knew You Were Waiting (For Me)', a duet with George Michael.

Aretha duetted with Al Green in 1995.

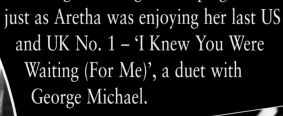

Aretha has sung with James Brown, Elton John, Whitney Houston, George Benson and the Eurythmics.

GOSPEL MUSIC

It's a testament to Aretha Franklin's extraordinary talent that she became a gospel star at such a young age. Gospel music is a huge movement amongst black Americans, so to stand out from the crowd, you need to offer something very special. Gospel services are joyous, celebratory and noisy events! Choirs praise the Lord through their music, with its striking harmonies and driving rhythms, usually accompanied by piano and percussion instruments.

Gospel music is an important part of the soul sound.

MARVIN GAYE

The Detroit-based company Motown launched some of the most talented, enduring and inspirational singers of the 20th century. No artist was more closely associated with that legendary label than Marvin Gaye, not least because he married the boss's sister! But neither Marvin's marriage nor his tenure at Motown were destined to last.

FRIENDS IN HIGH PLACES

Like Aretha Franklin, Marvin Pentz Gay was born into a church family (he added the 'e' to his surname in adulthood, emulating his hero Sam Cooke). A shy boy, Marvin was brought up strictly by his father, who was a church minister. He found comfort in music, showing a talent for piano and drums, as well as singing. In 1960, Marvin and his friend Harvey Fuqua left their group, the Moonglows, and moved to Detroit. Harvey became involved with Motown, and recruited Marvin as a session drummer for the label. Within a year, Marvin had married Anna Gordy, the sister of Motown's founder, Berry Gordy.

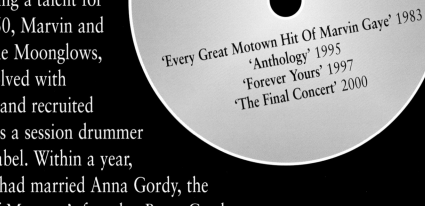

'What's Going On' 1971
'Let's Get It On' 1973
'Here My Dear' 1978
'Midnight Love' 1982

'Every Great Motown Hit Of Marvin Gaye' 1983
'Anthology' 1995
'Forever Yours' 1997
'The Final Concert' 2000

Marvin recorded 'Ain't No Mountain High Enough' with Tammi Terrell.

IT TAKES TWO

Marvin teamed up with a string of singing partners. After hits with Mary Wells and Kim Weston, he found his musical soulmate in Tammi Terrell. Nobody knows if Marvin and Tammi became lovers, but their intense musical intimacy is beyond doubt. Sadly, Tammi was dogged by ill-health, and she collapsed into Marvin's arms on stage. When she died in 1970, Marvin was so devastated that he became a recluse, and was rarely seen for the next year. His marriage to Anna was also crumbling at this time.

Marvin returned with a triumphant album, 'What's Going On', which he orchestrated and produced himself. There would be more hits in the '70s, but financial difficulties forced him out of America – he had debts of $7,000,000 by 1978. He settled in Ostend, Belgium, where he attempted to rebuild his life.

A VIOLENT END

Marvin was tempted back to the USA by a contract with Columbia, in 1982. The result was the album 'Midnight Love' and the award-winning single '(Sexual) Healing'. But this renewed success was short-lived. Years of drug abuse had left Marvin with paranoid delusions. He often threatened suicide and once had a gun forcibly removed from him. In 1984, the day before his 45th birthday, Marvin had a bitter argument with his father, whom he knew to be armed. The preacher shot his son dead, and was later sentenced to five years' imprisonment for manslaughter.

CIVIL RIGHTS

Soul music is closely linked to the civil rights movement. In the 1960s, black Americans supposedly had the same rights as white people, but there was still fierce racism and segregation, and many black people suffered a poor standard of living. Also, thousands of young Americans were being killed in the controversial Vietnam War. This led to anger and protest. Marvin Gaye reacted with a plea for tolerance and peace, in songs such as 'What's Going On' and 'What's Happening Brother'.

Martin Luther King was a civil rights campaigner. Marvin Gaye celebrated him in his song 'Abraham, Martin And John'. His birthday is now a US national holiday.

Marvin sometimes played keyboards on stage.

'I Heard It Through The Grapevine' is Marvin's best-known hit.

WHITNEY HOUSTON

Some people have all the luck. Whitney Houston is blessed with beauty, determination and an extraordinary vocal range. She was also born into a family with a matchless musical pedigree.

'Whitney Houston' 1985
'Whitney' 1987
'I'm Your Baby Tonight' 1990

'My Love Is Your Love' 1998
'Greatest Hits' 2000

RUNNING IN THE FAMILY

Whitney's mother is the soul singer Cissy Houston. Her cousin is another, more famous, vocalist, Dionne Warwick, so it was only natural that young Whitney should start singing from an early age. Her career began in a gospel setting – The New Hope Baptist Junior Choir. As a teenager, Whitney was already singing backing vocals for Chaka Khan and Lou Rawls, and developing a solo stage act.

'I Will Always Love You' won several Grammy awards.

SNAPPED UP

Whitney also pursued a modelling career, which saw her on the covers of several glossy magazines. This brought her to the attention of the head of Arista Records, who offered her a contract. Aided by some major songwriters, her first album sold an amazing 14 million copies.

RECORD-BREAKER

The follow-up, 'Whitney' shattered all records, by providing no fewer than seven No. 1 singles. It was difficult to avoid Whitney Houston in the 1980s – her music was on the radio, her videos were on television and her face was in every magazine. In 1992, Whitney added another string to her bow, by starring in an action film, 'The Bodyguard'. The love theme from the movie gave Whitney her biggest hit, 'I Will Always Love You', which spent 13 weeks at the top of the UK chart.

OVERDOING IT?

Many critics have accused Whitney of 'over-singing' – she rarely uses one note when five will do. But her fans don't seem to mind. Whitney still tours the world, accompanied by a vast entourage of assistants, and plays to packed arenas everywhere.

Whitney re-signed with Arista for $100,000,000 in 2001.

DIONNE WARWICK

Whitney Houston's cousin, Dionne Warwick, was one of the most famous singers of the 1960s, and the most successful interpreter of the songs of Burt Bacharach and Hal David. Dionne had hits with 'Walk On By', 'You'll Never Get To Heaven (If You Break My Heart)' and 'Do You Know The Way To San José'. She enjoyed a chart comeback in 1983 with the hit album 'Heartbreaker'.

Dionne topped the US chart with 'That's What Friends Are For' in 1985, with Elton John, Stevie Wonder and Gladys Knight.

Whitney married singer Bobby Brown in 1992.

The JACKSONS

One of the last great acts to appear on the Motown label was a group of five brothers from Gary, Indiana. In the early 1970s, the Jackson 5 were so huge that they even had their own TV cartoon series. Jackie, Tito, Jermaine and Marlon reunited in 2001, to play some concerts with their youngest brother, Michael – one of the biggest and most controversial stars in popular music, who has sold hundreds of millions of records.

BIRTH OF A LEGEND

The group first performed together in 1964, spurred on by their ambitious parents, who had spotted six-year-old Michael practising dance moves in front of a mirror. They gained a strong live reputation and won a number of talent contests. In 1969, they were signed by Motown boss Berry Gordy Jr, who moved them to Hollywood. 'I Want You Back', 'The Love You Save' and 'I'll Be There' were all No. 1 hits in America. Meanwhile, Michael started a successful solo career, while still a teenager.

SOLO SUCCESS

A move to Epic Records saw the band change their name to 'The Jacksons', with brother Randy replacing Jermaine. In 1979, Michael released his biggest hit to date, the album 'Off The Wall', which sold over 10 million copies. His follow-up was an even bigger hit – for nearly 20 years, 'Thriller' held the record as the biggest-selling album of all time. It also gave Michael the hit singles 'Billie Jean' and 'Beat It', 12 Grammy nominations and a record 37 weeks at the top of the US chart. But how do you follow a success like that? Michael's answer was to regroup with his brothers for the 'Victory' tour and album in 1984.

Michael Jackson is famous for his love of animals.

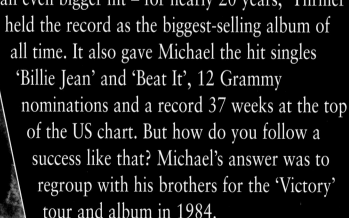

AN ECCENTRIC STAR

Michael nearly matched the sales of 'Thriller' with his 1987 album 'Bad', but as he grew older, his behaviour won him more headlines than his music. Eccentric to some, just plain weird to others, Michael surrounded himself with a variety of exotic pets at his lavish California mansion, complete with a working funfair in the garden! He has also undergone extensive plastic surgery, which has drastically altered his appearance, and even the colour of his skin seems to have changed. Michael caused an outcry at the 1996 Brit Awards in London, when he appeared to be emulating Jesus Christ in his stage act. Back in 2001 with 'Invincible', his first album of new material for many years, Michael topped the charts again, all over the world.

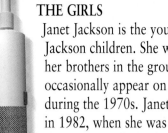

THE GIRLS

Janet Jackson is the youngest of the nine Jackson children. She was too young to join her brothers in the group, though she did occasionally appear on stage with them during the 1970s. Janet's first album appeared in 1982, when she was 16 years old. She was soon a star in her own right, renegotiating her record contract for millions of dollars. Her sister LaToya is the bad girl of the family. When her singing career stalled, LaToya wrote a controversial book, full of revelations about life in the Jackson household.

Janet Jackson is one of the biggest soul stars of the new millennium.

Jarvis Cocker of Pulp was so enraged by Michael Jackson's performance at the 1996 Brit Awards, that he invaded the stage, disrupting Michael's act.

The Jacksons:
'Diana Ross Presents The Jackson 5' 1970
'A B C' 1970
'Jackson 5 Christmas Album' 1970
'Victory' 1984

Michael Jackson:
'Off The Wall' 1979
'Thriller' 1982
'Bad' 1987
'Dangerous' 1992
'Invincible' 2001

WILSON PICKETT

The 'Wicked Pickett' was up there in the premier league of male soul singers, along with James Brown, Marvin Gaye and Otis Redding. He was the essence of macho, strutting, hip-grinding 1960s soul.

Wilson was signed to the Double L label by its founder, the singer Lloyd Price.

'In The Midnight Hour' 1965
'The Exciting Wilson Pickett' 1966

'Greatest Hits' 1976
'A Man And A Half' 1992
'It's Harder Now' 1999

PAYING HIS DUES

Wilson Pickett was born in Prattville, Alabama in 1941, and first came to prominence as the leader of the Detroit-based act the Falcons. Wilson was quickly signed as a solo artist by the small Double L label, and he had a handful of minor hits there. But his talents were spotted by the much larger Atlantic Records, and they bought out his contract.

MOVER AND SHAKER

Atlantic hooked Wilson up with ace producer Jerry Wexler, who took him to Stax studios in Memphis, to record with the soul band Booker T and the MGs. The result was 'In The Midnight Hour', which became a soul classic, covered by dozens of artists. '634-5789' followed in 1966, and spent seven weeks at the top of the R&B chart. Meanwhile, Wilson was honing his wild stage act with a large revue of musicians. The hits kept coming through the 1960s, including 'Mustang Sally' and a cover of the Beatles' 'Hey Jude'.

THE COMMITMENTS
Set in Dublin, 'The Commitments' is a movie about a group of young Irish musicians. Believing that the Irish have the same social standing in Europe as black people in America, they decide to start a soul band. This hilarious film follows the trials and tribulations they experience. The soundtrack album was almost as successful as the film. Lead-singer Andrew Strong belts out several soul classics, including the Wilson Pickett hits 'Mustang Sally' and 'In The Midnight Hour'.

Andrew Strong (third from right) was tipped for stardom after his role in 'The Commitments'.

A BAD MOVE
Many soul artists found that when they left Atlantic or Motown, the hits started to dry up. Wilson Pickett was no exception, and a move to RCA in 1973 saw a downturn in his fortunes. His aggressive stage persona was matched by a fiery temperament off-stage, fuelled by his passion for alcohol. In 1974, Wilson was arrested for pulling a gun during an argument. But for the next few years, he carried on doing what he knew best – leaping around on stage, growling and shrieking in a suggestive manner. Wilson signed to Motown for a time, and had some modest success, but his greatest achievements were in the 1960s and early '70s, all now beautifully preserved on CD.

Wilson Pickett toured constantly through the 1970s.

OTIS REDDING

In 1967, a small private plane inexplicably dived into a lake in Wisconsin. Amongst the dead was soul singer, Otis Redding, the greatest star to record for Stax.

'(Sittin' On) The Dock Of The Bay' sold over a million copies in the UK.

STAX BECKONS

Like so many other blues and soul performers, Otis started his career by winning talent competitions – not the ones in the famous Apollo Theater in Harlem, but in the Douglas Theater in Macon, Georgia. Through a school friend, Otis was introduced to his heroes, Johnny Jenkins and the Pinetoppers, and he happily accepted a job with them as a general assistant and occasional singer. In 1962, Otis drove the band to a session at the legendary Stax studios in Memphis. With some studio time left over, Otis persuaded Stax owner Jim Stewart to let him record two of his own compositions. Stewart was so impressed with the results that he released the first Otis Redding single, 'These Arms Of Mine', which hit No. 20 on the R&B chart.

A SECOND HOME IN HARLEM

'Pain In My Heart' 1964
'The Great Otis Redding Sings Soul Ballads' 1965
'Otis Blue' 1965
'Dock Of The Bay' 1968
'Otis Redding In Person At The Whiskey A Go Go' 1968
'Dreams To Remember – The Otis Redding Anthology' 1998

On the strength of his first few hits, Otis was offered a regular slot at the Apollo Theater in Harlem, and was paid $400 per week – a fortune. Otis continued to record and built up a reputation as a fine songwriter – Aretha Franklin took his song 'Respect' to the top of the charts in 1967. In 1965, he released 'Otis Blue', one of the greatest soul albums ever.

Otis astonished everyone at the June 1967 Monterey Pop Festival. His performance was seen as a deliberate attempt to capture the white rock audience. Otis was the only soul singer on a bill featuring rock acts such as Jimi Hendrix and the Who, but the hippy audience was knocked out by his energy and verve.

POSTHUMOUS LEGEND

On the 7th of December, Otis entered Stax studios to record his biggest hit, '(Sittin' On) The Dock Of The Bay', a relaxing ballad. But he would not live to see its success – just three days later he was dead. By the end of the decade, Otis's brand of gentle soul was out of fashion, but a loyal core of fans and a string of CD reissues have kept his music alive. Today, Otis's records sound as fresh as the day they were recorded.

THE MEMPHIS SOUND

Memphis, Tennessee was the home of Stax Records, one of the four major soul labels. Jim Stewart and his sister Estelle Axton were the owners of a Memphis record store, who decided to start their own label, Satellite, in 1959. Their first releases were records of country music, but because they were located in a black area of town, they soon switched to heavy R&B and soul. They changed their name to Stax in 1961, and had Sam and Dave, Eddie Floyd, Isaac Hayes and William Bell on their books.

Booker T and the MGs was Stax's resident session band.

Otis was only 26 when he died.

21

SMOKEY ROBINSON

William 'Smokey' Robinson would have been remembered as one of the chief figures in soul music, even if he had never sung a note. His writing for Motown acts, such as the Temptations, Marvin Gaye and Mary Wells, led Bob Dylan to name him 'America's greatest living folk poet'. But Smokey also possesses one of the most emotional voices in music.

The 'Motortown Revue' featured Martha and the Vandellas, the Supremes and Stevie Wonder, as well as the Miracles, with Smokey on lead vocals (above).

MOTOWN'S FINEST

Smokey Robinson and the Miracles were spotted by Motown boss Berry Gordy Jr in 1957. For the next decade, they recorded some of Motown's greatest hits, including 'I Second That Emotion', 'Tracks Of My Tears' and 'Tears Of A Clown'. All this time, Smokey was establishing himself as a highly sophisticated songwriter, whose blend of poignant lyrics and intricate melody provided hits for a string of artists. Smokey and the Miracles toured the world during the '60s, and were even hailed as the Beatles' favourite band.

ELECTED TO THE BOARD

In 1971, Smokey left the Miracles to concentrate on his position as vice-president of Motown, in charge of nurturing new talent. He claimed that he had no wish for a solo career, as he contined to produce the Miracles and write for other artists. But Smokey's 'retirement' did not last for long. His records in the 1970s tended to be more reflective and experimental than his earlier work, and though they rarely reached the heights of his '60s hits, they confirmed Smokey's reputation as soul's most thoughtful and intelligent artist.

BACK IN THE CHARTS AGAIN

It looked as though Smokey was going to ease gently into middle age, but it was not to be. In 1981, he scored a huge surprise hit with 'Being With You', which hit No. 1 nearly 25 years after he started in showbusiness. Smokey left Motown in 1990, but he still releases occasional records today, and plays to adoring fans all over America.

THE DETROIT SOUND

Motown is the best-known of all the major soul labels. It got its name from its home, Detroit, the centre of the American car industry – motor town. Berry Gordy Jr worked in a car factory in the mid-1950s, but he supplemented his income by writing songs and producing records. He launched Motown in 1960, and its subsidiary Tamla shortly afterwards. Motown's roster of artists included the Four Tops, the Marvelettes, Gladys Knight and the Pips, the Isley Brothers and the Supremes. Berry also wrote several songs with Smokey Robinson.

Berry Gordy Jr moved Motown to Los Angeles in 1970.

Smokey toured less frequently during the 1970s.

'A Quiet Storm' 1975
'Whatever Makes You Happy' 1993
'Ultimate Collection' 1997

'Intimate' 1999
'Along Came Love' 1999
'Our Very Best Christmas' 1999

DIANA ROSS

Singing groups come and go in pop music. Once they have gone their separate ways, it's rare for group members to repeat their earlier success. But when Diana Ross left the Supremes, the most popular girl group of the 1960s, she went on to a triumphant solo career, and became the biggest black female star of all time.

MAKING OF A DIVA

The Supremes often toured and recorded with their Motown labelmates, the Temptations.

Diana Ross had already enjoyed twelve US No. 1 singles with the Supremes when she left the group in 1970. She had been the focal point of the Supremes, and Motown boss Berry Gordy Jr had wisely been grooming her for solo stardom for some time. Diana made her debut solo performance just seven weeks after leaving the group. Six months later, she had her first solo No. 1, a re-arrangement of 'Ain't No Mountain High Enough', which had been a hit for Marvin Gaye and Tammi Terrell. Diana kept up a frantic recording schedule, and by the end of 1973, she had no fewer than seven hit albums to her name. Diana's records in the 1970s were usually richly arranged ballads, which were typical of the 1970s Motown sound.

LADY SINGS THE BLUES

During her early solo years, Diana Ross also forged a career as a film actress. She starred in 'Mahogany', for which she designed her own costumes – all 50 of them! She also appeared in 'The Wiz', a re-make of the classic movie 'The Wizard Of Oz'. But her most acclaimed performance was in 'Lady Sings The Blues' in 1972. Diana was nominated for an Oscar for her portrayal of Billie Holiday, the singer whose life was tragically cut short by addictions to drugs and alcohol.

Billie Holiday, or 'Lady Day', was only 44 when she died in hospital, under police guard for drugs offences.

STAYING ONE STEP AHEAD

Diana's music was always at the forefront of changing fashions in the 1970s. Her albums 'The Boss' and 'Diana' were heavily influenced by disco. As she entered the third decade of her career, Diana was still at the top end of the charts with 'Upside Down', 'My Old Piano' and 'It's My Turn'. Her final single for Motown was also the biggest hit the label had ever had – 'Endless Love', a duet with Lionel Richie.

'Diana Ross' 1970
'Everything Is Everything' 1971
'Lady Sings The Blues' 1973
'The Boss' 1979
'Diana' 1980

'Why Do Fools Fall In Love' 1981
'Swept Away' 1984
'Take Me Higher' 1995
'Every Day Is A New Day' 1999
'Love From Diana Ross' 2001

Diana Ross is a mother of five children.

Motown invested $100,000 in Diana's solo career.

THE BOSS TAKES CONTROL

The move from Motown in 1981 gave Diana a lucrative new recording contract. 'Why Do Fools Fall In Love', 'Chain Reaction' and 'Muscles' sold millions, but Diana's music was moving away from soul and into the realms of pure pop music. Today, Diana is admired as much for her elegance and keen business-sense, as for her singing. She remains the undisputed First Lady of soul.

IKE and TINA TURNER

There have been many acclaimed double-acts in soul. But none could match the raw excitement of the husband and wife team Ike and Tina Turner.

The Ike and Tina Turner Revue was legendary on the live circuit.

START OF THE MARRIAGE

Ike was already a well-known producer, writer, DJ and performer, when 16-year-old Annie Mae Bullock came to see him at a club in East St Louis, Missouri. After much persuasion, Ike agreed to give Annie Mae a turn on the microphone. Her dazzling, uninhibited performance won her the job of Ike's regular vocalist. Two years later, in 1958, the couple were married, and Annie Mae adopted the stage name Tina Turner. They scored a handful of hit singles in the early 1960s, but Ike and Tina were best known for their stunning stage show.

THE SPECTOR TREATMENT

In 1966, they met producer Phil Spector, who was eager to record Tina's voice. Spector was less impressed with Ike, and offered him $20,000 on the condition that he stayed away from the studio! The powerful and emotional single, 'River Deep, Mountain High', was a huge hit in the UK, but, to everyone's amazement, it was a flop in the USA. For Ike and Tina, it meant a return to their relentless life on the road.

LOVE ON THE ROCKS

Ike and Tina's blend of soul and hard rock won them many fans amongst 1970s audiences. 'Proud Mary' and 'Nutbush City Limits' were major hit singles, but by now their marriage was crumbling. Tina would later claim that Ike regularly assaulted her during this period, and in 1976, she finally found the courage to leave him. With four children to support and no regular income, Tina was forced to play cabaret shows to smaller and smaller audiences. By 1979, she was $500,000 in debt and without a record deal.

Tina Turner was still performing into her sixties.

THE COMEBACK QUEEN

Help arrived in the form of Roger Davies, a young Australian promoter, hungry to make it in the American music business. Tina agreed to pare down her band to give it a harder edge, and accepted supporting slots with some major rock bands. Davies worked hard to secure Tina a recording contract, and in 1984 her single 'What's Love Got To Do With It' hit the US No. 1 slot, 24 years after her first chart entry with Ike. Tina sold millions of records throughout the 1980s and '90s, sealing her reputation as a soul legend. Ike, meanwhile, continued to produce and record, in between spells in prison for fraud and drugs offences.

Tina duetted with Mick Jagger at Live Aid in 1985.

PHIL SPECTOR

Phil Spector is the most famous American record producer, and one of the most enigmatic figures in the music business. Phil started out with the Teddy Bears, who hit the top in 1958 with 'To Know Him Is To Love Him'. Phil spent the early 1960s developing his 'wall of sound' technique, by adding layer upon layer of orchestral instruments and backing vocals. After 'River Deep, Mountain High' flopped in America, Phil went into semi-retirement, emerging occasionally to produce the Beatles, Leonard Cohen and the Ramones.

Phil Spector was at the forefront of modern technology.

Ike and Tina Turner:
'The Soul Of Ike And Tina Turner' 1960
'River Deep, Mountain High' 1966
'Too Hot To Hold' 1975
'Proud Mary' 1991

Tina Turner:
'Private Dancer' 1984
'Break Every Rule' 1986
'Foreign Affair' 1989
'Twenty Four Seven' 1999

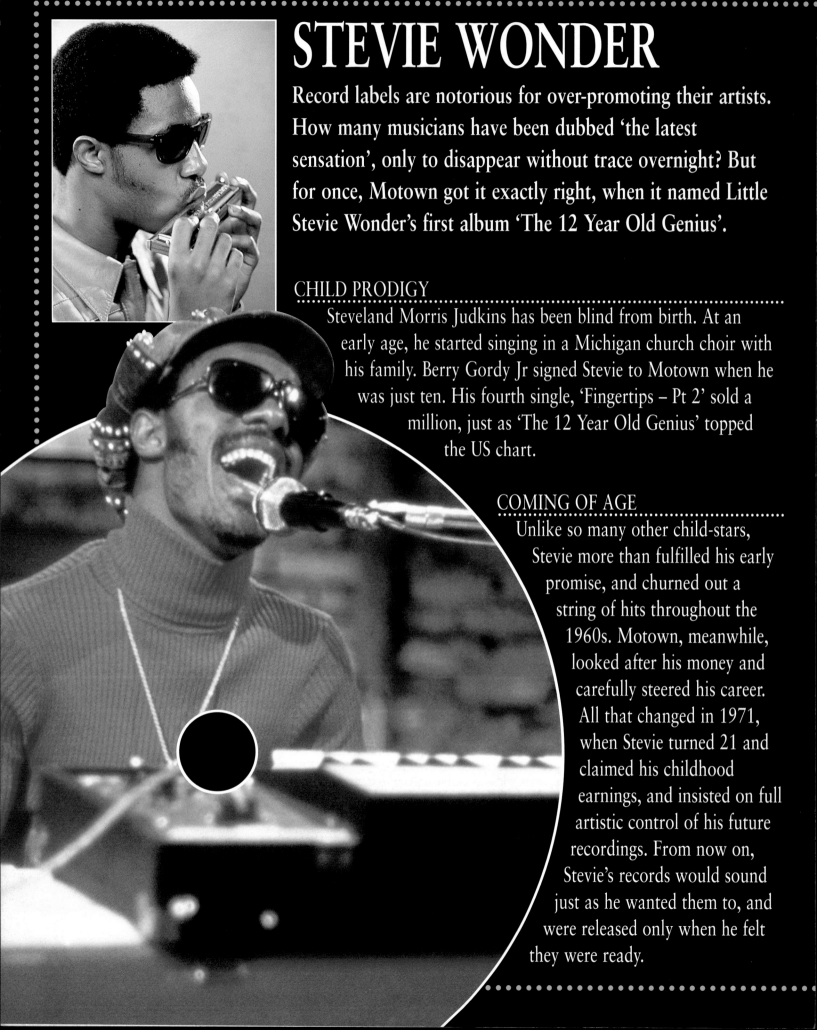

STEVIE WONDER

Record labels are notorious for over-promoting their artists. How many musicians have been dubbed 'the latest sensation', only to disappear without trace overnight? But for once, Motown got it exactly right, when it named Little Stevie Wonder's first album 'The 12 Year Old Genius'.

CHILD PRODIGY

Steveland Morris Judkins has been blind from birth. At an early age, he started singing in a Michigan church choir with his family. Berry Gordy Jr signed Stevie to Motown when he was just ten. His fourth single, 'Fingertips – Pt 2' sold a million, just as 'The 12 Year Old Genius' topped the US chart.

COMING OF AGE

Unlike so many other child-stars, Stevie more than fulfilled his early promise, and churned out a string of hits throughout the 1960s. Motown, meanwhile, looked after his money and carefully steered his career. All that changed in 1971, when Stevie turned 21 and claimed his childhood earnings, and insisted on full artistic control of his future recordings. From now on, Stevie's records would sound just as he wanted them to, and were released only when he felt they were ready.

Stevie is a harmonica- and keyboard-player, as well as a singer.

In late 1984, the Irish singer Bob Geldof was shocked by TV pictures of the devastating Ethiopian famine. He gathered the top British musicians of the day and recorded a charity single to raise money for the victims. America quickly followed suit with 'We Are The World', by USA For Africa, a collection of performers which included Harry Belafonte and Stevie Wonder. Both singles raised millions for the starving.

Lionel Richie, Dionne Warwick, Bob Dylan and many others sang 'We Are The World' at the Live Aid concert in July 1985.

TAKING THE REINS

Despite Motown's misgivings, Stevie delivered some of the classic soul recordings of the 1970s, and embraced the latest electronic technology. 'You Are The Sunshine Of My Life', 'He's Misstra Know It All', 'I Wish' and 'Sir Duke' have been covered by dozens of artists.

'For Once In My Life' 1968
'My Cherie Amour' 1969
'Signed, Sealed & Delivered' 1970
'Music Of My Mind' 1972
'Talking Book' 1972

'Innervisions' 1973
'Songs In The Key Of Life' 1976
'Hotter Than July' 1980
'In Square Circle' 1985
'At The Close Of A Century' 1999

MUSIC WITH A CONSCIENCE

Stevie was closely involved with disability and civil rights issues. His duet with Paul McCartney, 'Ebony And Ivory' celebrated racial harmony, and 'Happy Birthday' helped to persuade the American government to recognize Martin Luther King's birthday as a national holiday. Today, new releases from Stevie Wonder are increasingly rare, but the fiftysomething genius still has plenty to offer his fans over the next few years.

Stevie won an Oscar for 'I Just Called To Say I Love You' from the 1984 movie 'The Woman In Red'.

GAZETTEER

The huge success of soul stars such as Stevie Wonder and Whitney Houston sometimes overshadows the achievements of other, equally important, musicians. And great soul was not solely confined to the big four labels – Buddah, ABC Paramount, Vee-Jay, Mercury and Casablanca all produced some classic soul records.

The Isleys added two more brothers and a cousin, to make a five-piece band in 1969.

Curtis Mayfield founded his own Curtom label in 1968.

BROTHERLY LOVE

The Isley Brothers were one of the most successful and longest-lived soul groups. The original Isleys, Rudolph, Ronald and O'Kelly started singing gospel music in Cincinnati in the mid 1950s. But it was only in the late '60s and '70s that they achieved international success, with songs such as 'Behind A Painted Smile' and 'Harvest For The World'. The Four Tops have lasted even longer. The group formed in Detroit in 1953, and were still together, their line-up unchanged, nearly half a century later. The Impressions were formed in 1957, and still perform today. Their leader, Curtis Mayfield, left the group in 1970 and recorded the soundtrack to the 'blaxploitation' movie 'Superfly'. It topped the US chart for a month.

Hundreds of fans rioted at Sam Cooke's funeral in Chicago.

The Four Tops are still a popular concert attraction.

INSPIRATIONAL SINGER

Sam Cooke had one of the most romantic and wistful voices in soul. 'Only Sixteen', 'Wonderful World' and 'Cupid' enchanted a generation of listeners. Tragically, Sam was shot dead in 1964, in mysterious circumstances.

Like James Brown, Barry White served time in a corrective institution as a youth.

FEMALE SINGERS

Gladys Knight and the Pips were the first act to have a hit with 'I Heard It Through The Grapevine', later covered by Marvin Gaye. Singer Randy Crawford has made little impression in her native America, but in the UK and Europe, her records have sold millions, and her concerts never fail to sell out.

Randy Crawford's 'Secret Combination' album spent over a year on the UK chart.

SOUL GIANT

Barry White is a huge star, in more ways than one! Barry's rich bass voice perfectly complements his bulky physique, and his versions of 'You're The First, The Last, My Everything' and 'Just The Way You Are' had audiences swooning in the '70s.

Gladys Knight won $2,000 in a TV talent contest at the age of eight!

AWARD-WINNING SONGWRITER

The Commodores were one of Motown's most valuable acts in the 1970s. They owed much of their success to the singing and songwriting of Lionel Richie, who gave them 'Easy' and 'Three Times A Lady'. Lionel launched a solo career in 1982, and was king of the dancefloor with 'All Night Long' and the album 'Dancing On The Ceiling'.

The Commodores carried on after Lionel Richie (bottom centre) left the group.

31

INDEX

AC/DC 9
Atlantic 5, 8, 9, 11, 18, 19
Bell, William 21
Benson, George 11
Booker T and the MGs 5, 18, 21
Brown, James 6, 7, 11, 18
Burke, Solomon 9
Byrd, Bobby 6

Charles, Ray 5, 8, 9
Coasters, the 9
Cocker, Jarvis 17
Cole, Nat 'King' 8
Commitments, the 19
Commodores, the 31
Cooke, Sam 12, 31
Crawford, Randy 31

Davies, Roger 27
Dylan, Bob 22, 29

Ertegun, Ahmet 9

Falcons, the 18

Floyd, Eddie 21
Four Tops, the 23
Franklin, Aretha 5, 9, 10, 11, 12, 20
Fuqua, Harvey 12

Gaye, Marvin 12, 13, 18, 22, 24, 31
Gordy, Anna 12
Gordy, Berry 12, 22, 23, 24, 28
Green, Al 11

Hayes, Isaac 5, 21
Holiday, Billie 24
Houston, Cissy 14
Houston, Whitney 11, 14, 15, 30

Impressions, the 30
Isley Brothers, the 23, 30

Jackson 5 16, 17
Jackson, Janet 17
Jackson, LaToya 17
Jackson, Michael 16, 17

Jenkins, Johnny 20

Khan, Chaka 14
King, Martin Luther 13, 29
Knight, Gladys and the Pips 23, 31

Led Zeppelin 9
Live Aid 27, 29

Martha and the Vandellas 22
Marvelettes, the 23
Mayfield, Curtis 30
McCartney, Paul 29
Motown 5, 9, 12, 19, 24, 25, 28, 29

O'Jays, the 5

Pendergrass, Teddy 5
Pickett, Wilson 9, 18, 19
PIR 5, 9

Rawls, Lou 14
Redding, Otis 18, 20, 21
Richie, Lionel 25, 29, 31
Robinson, Smokey 5, 22, 23
Ross, Diana 24, 25

Sam and Dave 21
Spector, Phil 26, 27
Stax 5, 9, 18, 20, 21
Stewart, Jim 20, 21
Supremes, the 22, 23, 24

Temptations, the 22
Terrell, Tammi 12, 24
Three Degrees, the 5
Turner, Ike 26, 27
Turner, Tina 26, 27

Warwick, Dionne 14, 15, 29
Wells, Mary 12, 22
Weston, Kim 12
Wexler, Jerry 11, 18
White, Barry 31
Wonder, Stevie 5, 22, 28, 29, 30

PHOTOGRAPHIC CREDITS *Abbreviations: t-top, m-middle, b-bottom, r-right, l-left, c-centre.*

Cover m, 4-5, 6 both, 7tr, 8 both, 10tl, 12bl, 13mr, 20r, 21mr & bl, 22tl & ml, 24br, 26mr, 27tr, 30tl & br, 31br (Michael Ochs Archives) Cover bl, 21br, 23mr, 24tl & ml, 25bl, 26tl, 28 both, 30bl, 31m (RB) Cover bm, 3, 7bl, 9ml, 10b, 11br, 12tl, 13bl & br, 15br, 22br, 22-23, 29tl, 3tl (David Redfern) Cover br & 19br (NE/Reporta) 5tr & 31tr (Glenn A. Baker) 7tl (Robin Little) 9mr (Chuck Stewart) 9b (Paul Bergen) 11tr, 19tl, 27bl (Ebet Roberts) 11bl (Leon Morris) 14tl (JM International) 14bl (F.L. Lange) 14-15 (Michael Finn) 15tr & 17tr (Jon Super) 16tl (Harry Goodwin) 16bl (Fin Costello) 16mr (Grant Davis) 16-17 (Kieran Doherty) 18tl (Chuck Boyd) 18r (Crixpix) 20tl (CA) 25r (Diana Scrimgeour) 26br (Dan Smiley) 29mr (Richie Aaron) 29bl (Mick Hutson) 30tr (Gems) - Redferns. 19mr - The Kobal Collection.